# Important Note

This book provides pathways to investigate our behaviors, thoughts, emotions, etc. It should in no way replace an actual consultation with a doctor or health professional.

The information provided in this book in no way replaces traditional medicine or the healthcare recognized by the government institutions in your country.

This book, with its holistic approach, is only intended to complement the healthcare system in your country, and I encourage you to see a health professional for any health questions or concerns.

# Chakras for Kids

Ludi C.R.

I dedicate this book to
my two daughters,
R. and C.,
my two little angels
that inspire me every
day to journey towards
a better version of
myself.

# Chakras for Kids

## (and their parents!)

Ludi C.R.

# Dedication of love

I would like to dedicate this book to my daughters,
R. and C.

They are the ones who inspired me to explore another version of myself, to give meaning and new direction to my life, to discover who I am and to become a better person.

Though the road ahead is still long, I've committed myself to this path, to discover and become who I really AM...

Though the task may seem arduous, I know I will keep going, because the process makes me feel alive...

I do not know what direction my path will lead me... but I move forward with serenity and cheerfulness.

My daughters, I hope to share some of my journey with you, to make your own path easier, help you walk it earlier than I did, so you can begin to connect with your own inner BEING sooner.

May you live a life full of happiness and fulfillment, with all the wonders the Universe has to offer.

I have not always and will not always live up to your expectations, nor to my own as a mother, because I am far from perfect, I am human after all!

... But I hope you won't hold that against me...

I also hope I will know how to support you in identifying your inner SELF, your mission in your life, your life path, and being in tune with WHO you are.

I love you, I adore you...

May this book enlighten and inspire you in some way in this incarnation, as I hope I will succeed in fulfilling the purpose for which I was entrusted with your soul.

I love you.

Mom

Drawing done by my daughter, R., at (almost) 9 years old.
Thank you my Darling! ♥

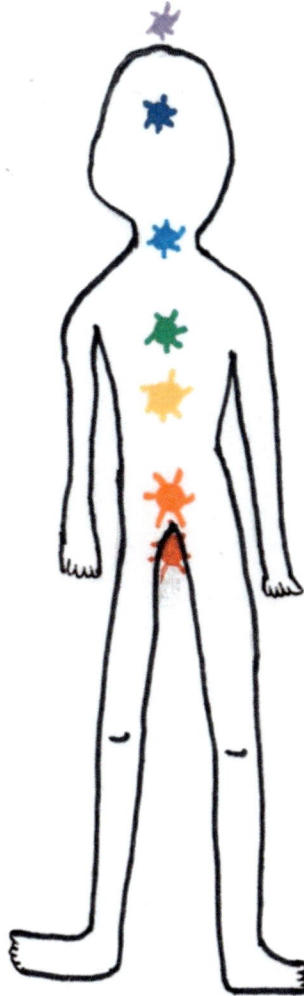

# TABLE OF CONTENT

# Acknowledgments

Dear parents and adults who have acquired this book for your children or to gift to others,

I hope it will meet your expectations and your child will find simple, clear, and understandable enlightenment on what chakras are.

This book is intended as an introduction – a summary – to allow a young child to learn about the existence of chakras, and provide them with some information that will get them interested – I hope – in learning more as they grow.

I hope this book will represent a legacy for our children, to support them at a younger age on their path to personal and spiritual development.

To support them earlier, when we as parents have often taken so long and waited until our forties (like me!) or later to go on our own adventure down the path of exploration and self-discovery.

I hope this book, and those that follow, will allow our children to benefit at a young age from knowledge and understanding that promotes development and self-awareness.

Young children may need an adult's assistance to read and understand this book.

This book provides a variety of information that the child can go back and reread, and will continue to understand better as they grow and reach their teenage years.

The first time reading it, children may only retain a few points and keywords, and will gradually increase their knowledge as they reread it again, and again. I invite adults to do the same.

I wish you all, adults, parents, and children, happy reading and a wonderful adventure...

Thank you with all my heart for reading this book...

# Introduction

# What are chakras?

Chakras are wheels of energy.

The word 'chakra' comes from the ancient Indian language "Sanskrit", and means "wheel of light".

So you can imagine your chakras as wheels or circles of light.

There are several dozen chakras.

Here we will talk about the 7 main chakras located on our body, all along the spine.

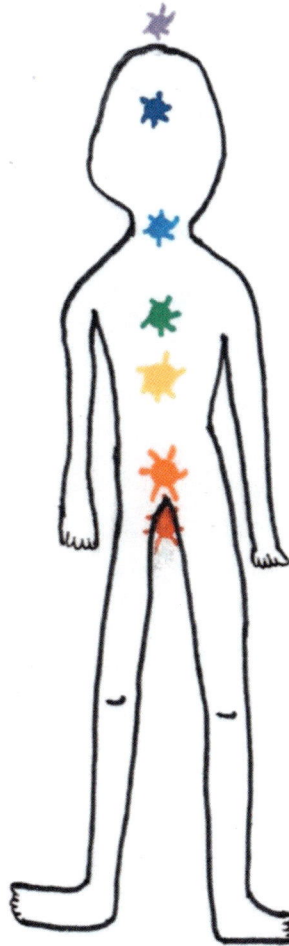

Chakras receive energy from the sky and earth, and distribute it to our bodies.

Our chakras are all dependent on one another.

If one chakra is weak, the other chakras will try to compensate; but this may weaken them in turn.

You can also imagine them as a system of interlocking gears. If one of them gets stuck, the whole system will be affected.

If our chakras are balanced, it is easier for us to manage our emotions, and our body remains in better health.

Conversely, if our emotions are too intense for a long period of time, or if our body is in bad health, our chakras may become unbalanced.

So, this can work both ways; imbalanced chakras can impact our body, our emotions, and our health.

And our body, our health and our emotions can impact the balance of our chakras.

"Negative" emotions (such as anger, fear, sadness, anxiety, etc.), as well as a bad diet (too much sugar and processed food, for example!) can block our chakras and prevent energy from circulating freely.

So, if a chakra gets stuck or turns weakly, energy cannot circulate correctly in our bodies.

If you want to take care of your chakras, you can easily do so just by trying to have positive thoughts and emotions, and eating healthy (vegetables and organic foods for example).

Having positive thoughts and emotions doesn't mean repressing your "negative" emotions.
It is important to express your feelings, let them "out", and ideally, to do so calmly.

In fact, if you repress your feelings, which means you don't listen to them or express them, you may end up shutting them into some part of your body where they will block the passage of energy.

So, if you are sad, or angry, or stressed, don't hesitate to say so.

Say so calmly.

For example, you can say "I feel anger inside of me... because...".

If you look carefully and understand where your feeling of anger, or frustration, or sadness, etc. is coming from... you can also try to make it go away, especially if you feel it in your body (such as a knot in your stomach due to stress).

You can then add, "I don't want this feeling of anger/fear/stress/etc. anymore... I understood what it was trying to tell me... Now I can let it go."

You will then feel the benefits in your body that come from freeing this emotion.

Did you know that every chakra is associated with an element, a color, and a music note?...

... You didn't?...

...Well let's discover all of them together...

# Presentation of the chakras

# The root chakra

# The 1st chakra: The root chakra

The 1st chakra is called the root chakra.

We saw in the beginning of this book that the word 'chakra' is from an ancient Indian language called Sanskrit.

In Sanskrit, the root chakra is called 'Muladhara'.

If you want, you can make it a game to memorize the Sanskrit names for chakras!

Each chakra also has a color. The root chakra is red.

Each chakra is also associated with a music note.
The root chakra is the music note C.

This chakra develops between the ages of 0 and 7 years old.

The root chakra is linked to the earth.

'Muladhara' is located at the base of the spine, at the coccyx.

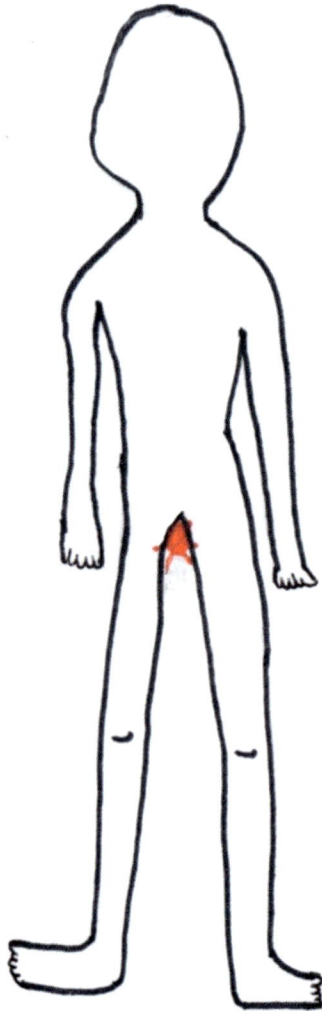

It conducts energy to the lower part of the body (the hips, the legs, and the feet), and anchors us to the Earth.

It's as if you had roots under your feet that help you stay rooted.

This is why the 1st chakra is called the 'root chakra'.

The root chakra provides us with our vital energy, the energy that will circulate in our body.

This is the seat of our survival.

If our chakra is balanced, we are properly anchored to the earth. We are independent and responsible.

The root chakra brings us security.
When we feel safe, we can move forward serenely and stay anchored.

When this chakra is well-balanced, it helps keep you rooted in the earth, in the planet, the physical material of this world. (If you are very young, this may sound a bit complicated!)

The root chakra invites us to love and take care of ourselves.

If we know how to adapt and change while respecting ourselves and others without submitting, then we become better.

The more stable our inner reality is, and the more we are anchored in the earth and therefore in material life, then the more we are flexible and know how to adapt to change (you may need a few more years to understand this!...But these explanations may be interesting to help the adult reading along with you to explain it to you).

This chakra seeks our survival: a roof over our heads, food and water, warmth, and so on.

**The root chakra promotes stability and safety.**

Conversely, if our chakra is unbalanced, we lack energy and strength in our life.

So, when this chakra is in excess, we manifest aggressiveness, anger, violence, and jealousy.

When it is underactive, we manifest fear and worry towards life.

When we feel insecure, we fear for our existence, our life, and we lose energy.

So, it is important to feel safe deep down, so the root chakra remains active even during times of doubt, and maintains its balance.

The fear that comes from insecurity blocks the root chakra.

## Let go of your fears

So, if you feel afraid, don't hesitate to say so.

For example, you could say "I feel that I am afraid of... because...".

And you can add, "I don't want this feeling of fear any longer... I understand what it wanted to tell me... Now, I will let it go".

You can also repeat positive affirmations to yourself every day, such as "I love life".

By repeating them every day and believing in them, they will become your reality.

Be careful: really believing them, feeling them in your body and heart, is very important for your thoughts and words to become reality.

Saying it mentally without really believing it, won't bring you anything.

If the root chakra had to be summed up in one word, it would be the verb "to survive".

I survive, I live, I am.

# The sacral chakra

# The 2nd chakra: The sacral chakra

The 2nd chakra is called the sacral chakra.

It is known as 'Svadhisthana' in Sanskrit.

Its color is orange.

Its music note is D.

This chakra develops between the ages of 7 and 14 years old.

The sacral chakra deals with our **well-being** and **physical health**.

The sacral chakra is located about 5 cm under the navel.

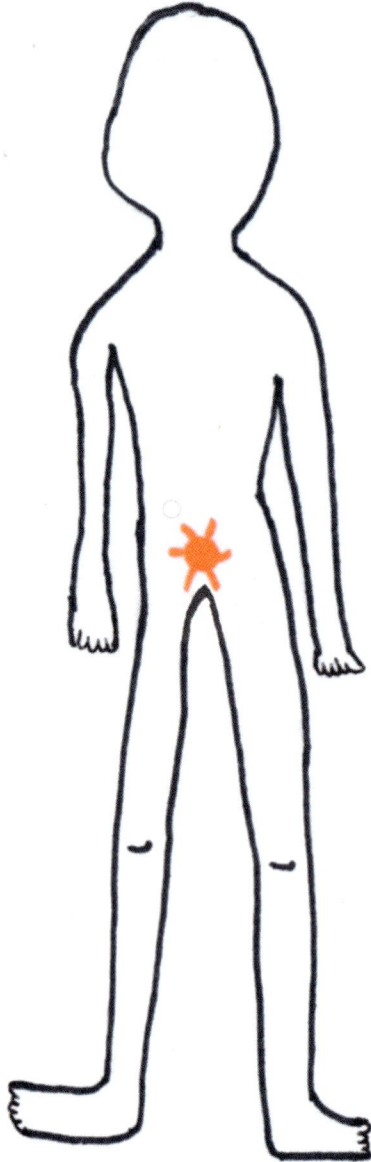

While the root chakra is linked to the earth, the sacral chakra is linked to water.

**It is the chakra of pleasure** (doing what you love and enjoying it).

In order to balance this chakra, it is important to take care of your body by eating healthy, doing sport, and having fun (creative activities, cooking, etc.).
It is also important to rest.

The little pleasures in life will help you keep your sacral chakra balanced, things like health and balanced meals, physical exercise, proper rest, and so on.

In this way you will continue to feed your sacral chakra's energy, even when it decreases during very stressful times.

Conversely, if this chakra is unbalanced, we are unsatisfied, we don't know what gives us pleasure.

The sacral chakra is blocked by guilt.

When we don't dare to express our emotions, and we repress them, they accumulate in our body, block it, and prevent it from thriving.

You can repeat positive affirmations every day, such as: "I love my body and I take care of it".

Accept your past actions, and forgive yourself.
Be good to yourself, and do not criticize yourself.

**The sacral chakra is linked to pleasure, to well-being, and to joy** if it is balanced. But if it is unbalanced, it leads to unhappiness.

If the sacral chakra had to be summed up in one word, it would be the verb **"to feel"**.

# The solar plexus chakra

# The 3rd chakra: The solar plexus chakra

The 3rd chakra is called the solar plexus chakra.

The solar plexus chakra is also known as 'Manipura' in Sanskrit.

Its color is yellow.

Its music note is E.

This chakra develops between the ages of 14 and 21 years old.

The 3rd chakra is located at the stomach, between your ribs.

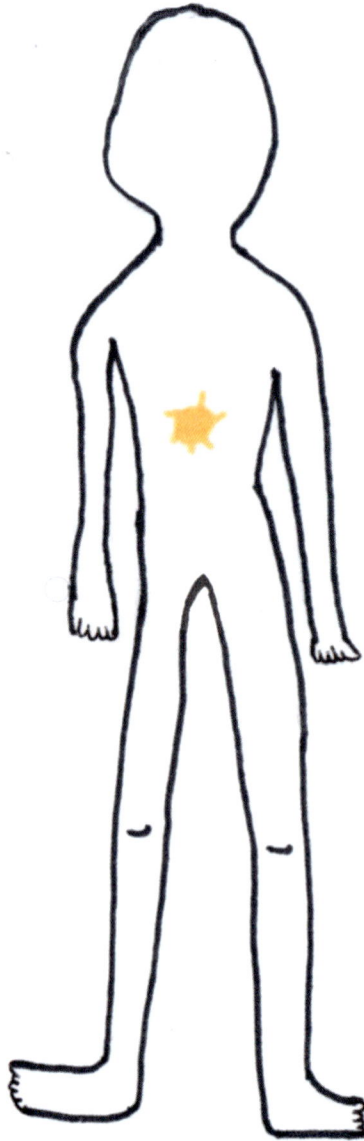

The 3rd chakra is associated with fire.

It is the seat of our willpower.

It deals with our **personality** and our **ability to radiate** who we are.

You can imagine it as a great big sun shining inside of you.

This chakra invites you to **become aware of your value.**
It reveals your personal power, your ability to choose.

**The 3rd chakra is associated with self-confidence, personal power, and freedom of choice.**

Throughout adolescence, we learn to respect who we are and assert our personality.

If our chakra is balanced, we have confidence (in ourselves, in life).
We are able to express who we are.
We are creative.
We are brave.

When this chakra is balanced, we assert our power to be ourselves in a healthy way, without going to excesses.

When this chakra is balanced, we assert who we are, we elicit respect from others in their behavior towards us, and we make appropriate choices for ourselves.

We activate the fire of our chakra, our inner fire, and in this way, we create important energy reserves.

When this chakra is unbalanced, we either seek to dominate others, or we become submissive:

When this chakra is too high, we seek to dominate others.

When this chakra is underactive, we adopt a submissive behavior; we become submissive and seek the recognition and approval of others.
We bend and submit to others.

If the solar plexus chakra is balanced, you will have confidence. Conversely, if it is unbalanced, you will show either submissive behavior or dominant power.

The solar plexus chakra is blocked by shame.

You can repeat – daily and with conviction – positive affirmations such as "I **radiate with all my being**".

Do not deny this part of yourself.

The verb associated with the solar plexus chakra is the verb "**to radiate**".

# The heart chakra

# The 4th chakra: The heart chakra

The 4th chakra is the heart chakra.

It is known as 'Anahata' in Sanskrit.

Its color is green.

Its music note is F.

This chakra develops between the ages of 21 and 28 years old.

The heart chakra is located in the middle of the chest.

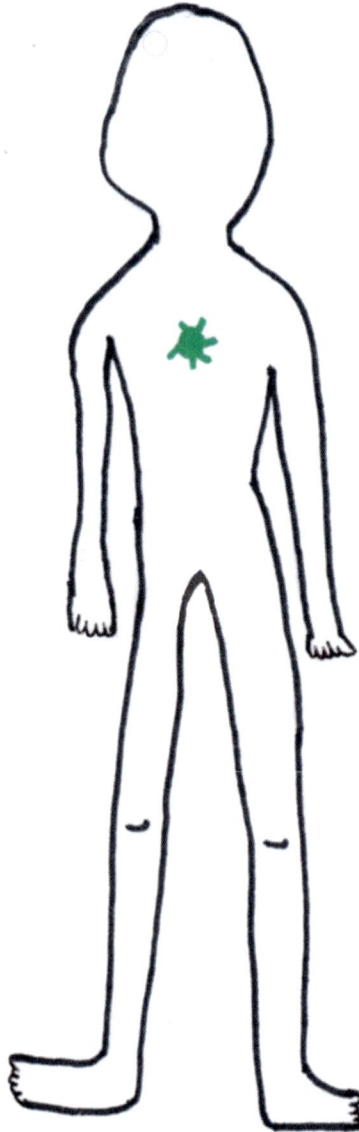

The heart chakra is the **seat of love.**

It refers to love: **love for yourself and love for others.**

**Love is an energy that circulates all around us.**

The heart chakra evokes **peace, joy and love.**
I love and accept to be loved.

When we see life as beautiful and positive, we allow our heart chakra to experience love and joy.

In order to balance your chakra, it is important to have happy, joyful, relaxing moments, to do activities that bring you pleasure, to spend time in nature, to spend pleasant moments with the people you love, and so on.

If our chakra is balanced, we are generous and loving.
We share. We love to help others and make ourselves useful.

If our chakra is unbalanced, we do not know how to love.
We only love conditionally.
We do not share with others and do not want to help them.
We build a shell around our heart to avoid suffering if we have been hurt.

The heart chakra is blocked by grief.

Every day you can repeat a positive affirmation such as "**I am love. I love, and am loved.**"

As always, try to repeat these affirmations with feeling and emotion, feeling them in your body and heart.

If your heart chakra is unbalanced, let go of your pain.
Love yourself and love others.

The verb associated with the heart chakra is the verb **"to love"**.

# The throat chakra

# The 5th chakra: The throat chakra

The 5th chakra is called the throat chakra.

It is known as 'Vishuddha' in Sanskrit.

Its color is sky blue.

Its music note is G.

This chakra develops between the ages of 28 and 35 years old.

It is located at the throat.

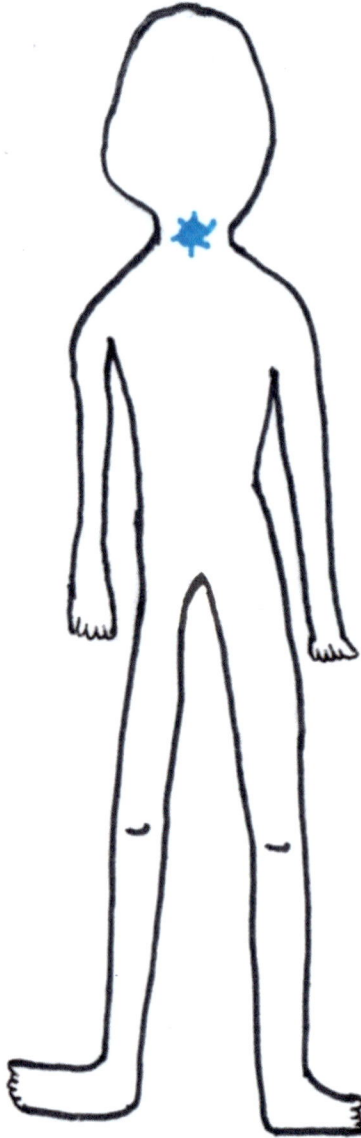

The throat chakra is associated with sound.
It is the **seat of truth**.

To develop this chakra, we can **sing, laugh, say** whether we are happy or not... **express ourselves**.

If our chakra is balanced, this means we say what we think.
We express our thoughts and emotions.

Situations don't stay stuck "in our throat".

If we tell the truth, we allow our throat chakra to develop.

It is important to learn to say what we think and feel, while being careful with our choice of words so we do not hurt others.

If our chakra is unbalanced, this means we don't dare speak and express ourselves.

We keep everything inside of us.

When we do not express our sadness, our anger, our suffering, our fear, etc., then our throat chakra may be blocked.

Similarly, if we speak badly about others, or if we consume unhealthy products (alcohol, tobacco, etc.), then our throat chakra may be affected (but you're a little young for that!).

If we lie, our throat chakra also tends to close up.

Our throat chakra can be blocked by the lies we tell ourselves, because we don't dare speak and express ourselves.

It may also be blocked by the lies we tell others.

But don't worry! Even though it's not a nice thing to lie, a little white lie here and there isn't going to block your throat chakra!

However, if you find yourself lying very often... you might want to think about stopping...

You can say this affirmation every day: "I communicate with others, I talk to them, I speak my truth, and I listen to them".

The verb associated with the throat chakra is the verb "to communicate".

# The third eye chakra

# The 6ᵗʰ chakra: The third eye chakra

The 6ᵗʰ chakra, the frontal chakra, is known as the third eye chakra.

It is known as 'Ajna' in Sanskrit.

Its color is dark blue.

Its music note is A.

This chakra develops between the ages of 35 and 42 years old.

The 6ᵗʰ chakra is located between the two eyebrows.

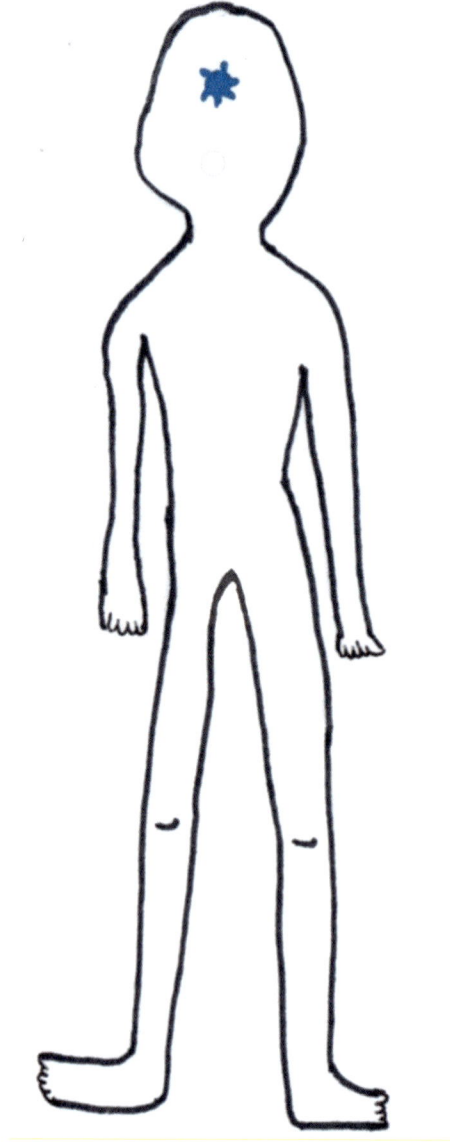

The third eye chakra is the **seat of interiority**.

We live under the illusion of separation, of duality, when in fact we are all ONE and connected.

And yet, we live as if we were separate.
(yikes! This is complicated!).

Don't worry, your journey and development in life will allow you to understand this gradually.

**Ajna deals with the way we view life.**
So, if you **see life "through rose-colored glasses", you will strengthen Ajna.**

If our chakra is balanced, we try to be WISE (wisdom), and adapt to situations and events in our life.

If our chakra is unbalanced, we may lack humor and be too attached to things.

We may also be close-minded.

We have the right to experience our feelings, even if they don't seem like good ones.

We just need to choose the right words to express what we feel without hurting others.

To develop Ajna, you can try to imagine the life you want to live, and try to see the positive side in everything and every situation.

Conversely, if you only see the negative side of things, Ajna will weaken.

As a french song goes – if you don't know it, maybe your parents can have you listen to it – adopt a **"positive attitude"**!

Our thoughts are like magnets; positive thoughts attract positive situations, while negative thoughts attract negative situations.

So, try to be confident and think positively, and reassure your worries and fears.

The third eye chakra is blocked by illusion.

You can affirm, for example, "**I see the best in me, in others, and in every situation**".
This doesn't mean you should let yourself be bullied or taken advantage of... You should also know and respect your limits and have clear limits on what you will accept.

The verb associated with the third eye chakra is the verb "**to see**".

# The crown chakra

# The 7th chakra: The crown chakra

The 7th chakra is called the crown or coronal chakra.

The crown or coronal chakra is also known as 'Sahasrara' in Sanskrit.

Its color is violet.

Its music note is B.

This chakra develops between the ages of 42 and 49 years old.

This chakra is located on top of the head.

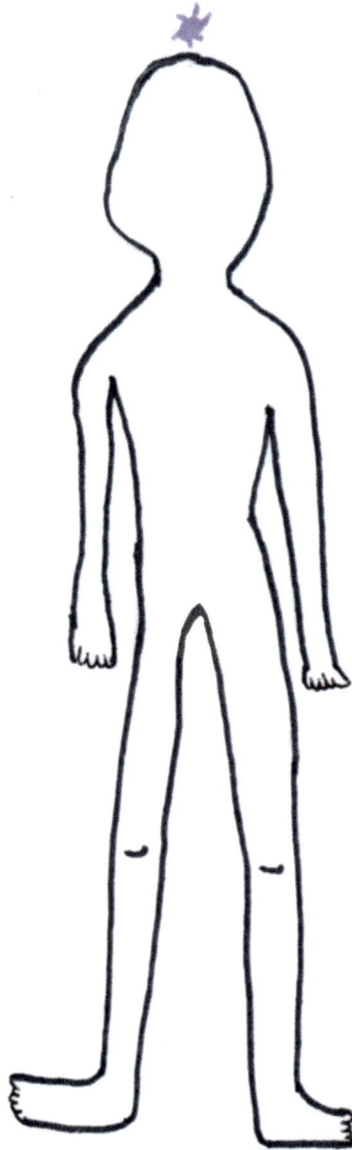

Sahasrara is linked to the mind.

The crown chakra is the seat of cosmic energy (the energy that comes from the cosmos, the universe).
It links us to the divine.

We understand that we are a divine being, and that we have become what we are through life and the difficulties and trials we have faced.

We understand that God (or whichever name you call your Deity or the Universe) protects and accompanies us on our journey, and we entrust ourselves to God's omnipotence.

We give ourselves over to the Universe and trust it.

The crown chakra invites us to **see with the love of the heart and the intelligence of the mind.**

When our crown chakra is open, we understand that we are protected by a higher power, a divine power.

If our chakra is balanced, we are thankful for everything we receive, every situation that occurs.

**We are thankful** for every event and situation that happens to us, and we live with **gratitude**.

To the contrary, if our chakra is unbalanced, we are inflexible and very selfish.

These are the earthly attachments that block the coronal chakra.

To balance our crown chakra, we should seek to be thankful for everything and live blissfully.

We should accept to entrust our sorrows and worries to a universal power.

You can, for example, repeat this affirmation: "I trust the universe to guide me and show me the next step to take on my journey".

The verb associated with the crown chakra is the verb "to be".

# Other ideas to harmonize your chakras

# Other ideas to harmonize your chakras

On the following page, you will find several ideas that you can have fun practicing regularly, to help harmonize your chakras.

# Meditation

# Meditation

Meditation calms your mind and allows you to listen to what your body is telling you.

By emptying your mind, you give yourself many more chances to hear the messages of the universe, of the angels, of guides, of your intuition... But this can take a lot of time and practice, so don't rush it...

Meditation can help you when you sense that your feelings are making you unhappy, when you are sad or have a knot in your stomach, etc.

Meditation helps calm you, and let go of the emotions that are disturbing your body, and to feel well again.

Here is a little exercise you can try every day in your room before going to bed, or any time you want to let go of negative emotions:

Lie down on your bed, or sit on a cushion on the ground with your legs crossed.

Close your eyes.

Breathe in gently and slowly, and feel your stomach swelling.

Breath out slowly and gently, and feel your stomach shrinking.
Do this 3 times.

Then, focus on each part of your body, from the top of your head down to your toes, including your arms and hands.

Take the time to travel slowly down from the top of your head to your toes, and to feel each part of your body as your attention travels down the length of your body.

If you don't feel anything, that's okay; you're feeling nothingness, and that's a good thing.

Little by little, you will start to feel things, very slowly and with practice.
It may be warmth or cold, tingling, your stomach growling, etc.

Just listen to what is happening in your body and what you are feeling, without any expectations.

Just observe...

You will now meditate on each chakra.

You can start with your root chakra.

Imagine a wheel of red light swirling and radiating around the root chakra.

This wheel spins clockwise (ask mom or dad if you're not sure which direction that is), and moves down towards the earth.

You can imagine this wheel connected to the center of the earth, and the heart of the earth nourishing you with its energy.

You feel happy, confident, and safe.

You can do this as long as you want or feel the need to.

Next, when you feel ready, you can move to your sacral chakra, and imagine a wheel of orange light coming out of your sacral chakra and growing every time you breathe in.
It expands and nourishes you with its joy and creativity.

Imagine that this wheel of light is spinning clockwise.

Again, focus and meditate on your sacral chakra as long as you want or feel the need to.

Next, you can meditate on the solar plexus chakra, and imagine a wheel of yellow light coming out of this chakra.

This wheel of light grows with every breath in.

It fills you with self-confidence.

When you feel confident enough, you can then move on to meditate on your heart chakra.

Imagine a wheel of green light coming out of your heart chakra, and growing with each breath in.

This wheel fills you with love as it grows.

You can sense the feeling of love growing in you.

Emotions of peace and joy fill your heart.

When you feel completely full of this joy and love, you can then choose to meditate on your throat chakra.

Imagine a wheel of sky-blue energy spinning clockwise as it comes out of your throat chakra.

It grows with each breath you take, and allows you to express yourself with calm and serenity.

You feel at ease expressing your thoughts and emotions.

You let your words out.

When you feel ready, you can meditate on your third eye chakra.

Just like the other chakras, you can imagine a wheel of dark blue light coming out of your third eye chakra, and growing with each breath you breath in.

This wheel allows you to see the positive side of life.

When you feel positive about life, you can then meditate on the crown chakra and imagine a violet-colored wheel growing with each breath and connecting you to the immenseness of the universe.

When you feel full of gratitude and thankfulness for life, and you are confident about the path ahead of you, you can choose to end your meditation session.

In the introduction to chakras, we looked at the positive affirmations you can repeat.

You can also repeat these during your meditation.

Also, if you want, you can choose to meditate on a single chakra.

You don't necessarily have to meditate on all of them every time.

You will know how many to do based on your needs, your feelings, and how much time you have...

There are many books available on meditation.

Perhaps you can ask your parents to find you some.

Some books also come with a CD... these can help you train and practice.

An adult can also practice meditation with you; it will benefit them too!

# Positive affirmations for the chakras

# Positive affirmations for the chakras

Every day, you can also recite affirmations to balance your chakras.

Here are a few examples, but you can write your own phrases, alone or with the help of your mom or dad.

I love myself

I love others, and I like to be loved

I say what I think and feel, without hurting others

I am in harmony with who I am

I like to make myself happy

I listen to what my body tells me

I like to walk and wander in nature

I feel good, calm, and happy

I appreciate the moments of... (pleasure, relaxation, fun, adventure, meals with family, etc.)

I like to share

...and so on.

As you can see, it is very important to feel the statement and speak it with emotion.

If you just think it in your mind, it is unlikely that it will bring you what you hope.

Don't choose too many phrases; you only need a few.

Even one phrase can be of huge benefit if formulated and expressed well.

You can ask mom or dad to help you form your sentence based on what you feel like expressing.

# A wide variety of other methods to harmonize chakras

There are many other ways to balance chakras (meditation, artistic activities, lithotherapy, etc.).

This book is not intended to introduce all of them, but you can read other books about these topics to find out more.

As you grow and read more along your journey, you will discover these other methods in more detail, and you can choose and retain the ones that fit you best.

# Thank you....

**I'd like to thank you....**

I'd like to thank you – and thank the adult who helped you read this – for having chosen this book.

This book is intended as an introduction to chakras, to allow the youngest among us to learn these teachings that are only now becoming popular across our continent.

And despite being just an introduction to the energies of chakras, I hope you (and the adult who helped you) found this book interesting.

I hope you will reread this book from time to time, especially the parts that interested you the most, and that you will think about it and put it into practice from time to time, or even better, regularly.

I hope this book helps you along your path, and has made you interested in your inner development.

I wanted to support my daughters in their spiritual growth and development.

So, I began to search for ways to share with them the knowledge I'd learned on my own recent journey, and how to transmit the information I now know about chakras and their meaning – a subject they would sometimes ask me about.

Not finding any book that dealt with this topic for children, I realized I could write my own...

I hope you and your child will enjoy reading this book as much as I enjoyed writing it...

If you are reading and enjoying this book, I'd be very grateful if you'd take the time to give it a 5-star rating! 😃 😍 😉

If you would like to help me improve my writing, please feel free to contact me and share your feedback by writing to ludi.cr@outlook.com.

Thank you for reading this book, I am very grateful.

# EVERYTHING

## has beauty

### but not everyone sees it.

Confucius

# About the author

I would like to dedicate this book to my daughters, R. and C.

They are the ones who inspired me to explore another version of myself, to give meaning and new direction to my life, to discover who I am and to become a better person.

Though the road ahead is still long, I've committed myself to this path, to discover and become who I really AM...

Though the task may seem arduous, I know I will keep going, because the process makes me feel alive...

I do not know what direction my path will lead me... but I move forward with serenity and cheerfulness.

My daughters, I hope to share some of my journey with you, to make your own path easier, help you walk it earlier than I did, so you can begin to connect with your own inner BEING sooner.

May you live a life full of happiness and fulfillment, with all the wonders the Universe has to offer.

I also hope I will know how to support you in identifying your inner SELF, your mission in your life, your life path, and being in tune with WHO you are.

May this book enlighten and inspire you in some way in this incarnation, as I hope I will succeed in fulfilling the purpose for which I was entrusted with your soul.

Made in the USA
Las Vegas, NV
12 October 2022